Apps and Integrations
Extending Microsoft Teams

Dr. Patrick Jones

OLYMPUS ACADEMY
PRESS

The Microsoft Teams Companion Series

The Microsoft Teams Companion Series

Welcome to *The Microsoft Teams Companion Series*—your step-by-step guide to mastering every aspect of Microsoft Teams. Each book in this collection covers a distinct area, ensuring that by the end, you'll possess an in-depth, holistic understanding of Teams for personal use, business, education, or enterprise-level deployments.

Here's what you'll find in this series:

1. *Introduction to Microsoft Teams*

2. *Teams & Channels*

3. *Chats & Meetings*

4. *Teams Phones*

5. *Apps & Integrations*

6. *Copilot in Microsoft Teams*

7. *Accessibility in Microsoft Teams*

8. *Microsoft Teams in Education*

9. *Security, Compliance, and Administration in Microsoft Teams*

10. *Expert Tips & Troubleshooting: Becoming a Microsoft Teams Power User*

Looking to dive even deeper into the Microsoft ecosystem? Explore our other companion series—*The Microsoft 365 Companion Series, The Microsoft Intune Companion Series, and The Microsoft Purview Companion Series*—all available on Amazon. Each provides the same clear, comprehensive coverage you'll find here, helping you expand and refine your skills across the full spectrum of Microsoft products and services.

TABLE OF CONTENTS

CHAPTER 1: WHY APPS AND INTEGRATIONS MATTER

Modern workplaces rely on more than just emails and meetings to get things done. Employees jump between file-sharing platforms, project management boards, chat apps, and countless browser tabs—making it easy to lose track of essential tasks or information. Microsoft Teams aims to reduce this friction by serving as a central hub, not just for messaging and calls, but also for a wide range of apps and integrations. By weaving your key tools directly into Teams, you can streamline everyday workflows, keep projects visible, and avoid the chaos of switching between multiple windows. In this opening chapter, we'll discuss why these apps matter, outline the different types of integrations in Teams, and preview what you'll learn throughout this book. Finally, we'll see how Sarah, a regular office professional, discovers the potential of merging her scattered tools into one platform.

In the past, employees typically used separate programs for different tasks—email for communication, a standalone project management site for tracking tasks, a web-based file repository for storing documents, and maybe a separate scheduling tool for events. Each solution lived in its own silo. If you needed to share an update in your project management app, you'd toggle away from the chat window, log in, find the relevant item, make your notes, then jump back to chat to confirm you'd updated it. These continuous "context switches" burn mental energy and can lead to details slipping through the cracks.

Apps and integrations in Microsoft Teams minimize that problem. They embed external tools into the same interface where you chat and host meetings. If your team uses Trello for tasks, you can add a Trello tab

1

inside a Teams channel. Instead of opening a separate browser tab every time you want to see or edit tasks, you click the channel tab and see your board right there. Or if you prefer a bot-based approach, you might install a bot that pulls updates from your bug-tracking system into a conversation, so no one has to manually copy-paste statuses. The result is fewer interruptions, faster updates, and a smoother flow of information.

Apps in Teams aren't just tacked-on extras. They're part of a broader Microsoft 365 ecosystem. For instance, your organization might already use Outlook for email, OneDrive for cloud storage, or SharePoint for intranet sites. Teams weaves these services together by letting you pin specific documents, embed lists or libraries, or even create custom solutions using the Power Platform. Meanwhile, thousands of third-party developers have built tools for everything from design feedback to daily stand-up reminders. Each integration aims to solve a particular need—like summarizing data from a CRM, polling your coworkers about a meeting time, or automatically creating tasks in Planner when someone posts a certain keyword in a channel.

As Microsoft continues expanding the 365 suite, new services often show up in Teams quickly—like Microsoft Loop components or advanced analytics from Viva Insights. This ecosystem is always shifting. By understanding how apps fit into Teams, you'll be ready to adopt new features or integrate emerging platforms, staying ahead of the curve in digital collaboration.

Within Teams, you'll see various ways third-party or Microsoft-native apps can appear:

1. Tabs: These let you display a web-based tool or page inside a channel, chat, or meeting. For example, you could create a "To Do" tab linking to Microsoft To Do or embed a Trello board under a "Planner" tab. Tabs make sure you don't need to leave Teams to see essential info—like a Kanban board or a report.

2. Bots: Chatbots live in Teams and can respond to commands or trigger notifications. A bot might fetch data from your CRM

when you type "@SalesBot get client record," or post daily reminders about tasks. Bots can be friendly Q&A helpers, pulling knowledge base info for employees who ask, "@HelpBot how do I request time off?"

3. Connectors: These push updates from external services into a Teams channel. For instance, if you connect your GitHub account, each new pull request or issue might post a short summary in your "Dev" channel. Connectors help the team track real-time changes without manually forwarding them.

4. Messaging Extensions: These appear at the bottom of your chat window, letting you insert content from another app directly into your conversation. For example, if you have a messaging extension for an app like YouTube or Microsoft Forms, you could click the extension's icon, search for a relevant video or create a quick poll, and drop it into the chat. Extensions reduce friction by letting you fetch data from external apps without leaving Teams.

Teams supports a vast App Store with third-party integrations like Asana, Trello, Salesforce, or even specialized industry apps (like service ticketing platforms). Microsoft also produces first-party solutions—like Planner, Power Automate, or Microsoft Whiteboard—that naturally tie into the 365 environment. The choice between third-party or Microsoft-first often depends on your existing tools, cost, or feature preferences. Some third-party apps can be more robust if you rely heavily on them, while Microsoft-first apps might integrate deeper with your user accounts, security, and data storage. In practice, many organizations blend both, installing official Microsoft apps (like Forms or Stream) plus a few specialized external ones.

In this book, you'll see:

• Governance and Security: How to manage which apps users can install, ensure data compliance, and define permission scopes. A well-intentioned user might add a random connector that posts sensitive info outside your domain, so a governance strategy keeps everything safe and consistent.

- Power Platform Ties: Microsoft's low-code tools—Power Apps, Power Automate, Power BI, and Power Virtual Agents—connect seamlessly with Teams. We'll explore how to build custom workflows, embed dashboards, or create simple apps that live inside a channel.

- Custom Development: If your business needs a unique tool or integrates with a proprietary system, you can develop a custom Teams app or bot. We'll look at the basic steps for building, testing, and deploying these custom solutions, even if you're not a heavy coder.

- Real-World Automation: We'll show examples of how automations can reduce repetitive tasks—like approving requests or generating weekly reports—so you can focus on higher-level work. Sarah's stories will demonstrate practical scenarios like an HR department automating onboarding steps or a marketing team building a quick poll bot for campaign updates.

By the end, you'll have the confidence to expand your Teams usage beyond simple chat or calls. You'll know how to bring external data in, push updates out, and even craft your own integrated workflows that lighten everyone's workload and keep collaboration transparent.

Realizing the Need to Unify Tools

At 365 Strategies, Sarah's marketing team juggled multiple sites and software daily—Microsoft Whiteboard for brainstorming, Trello for tasks, a separate time-tracking app, not to mention Outlook for email and, of course, Teams for chats and meetings. This scattering of tools led to occasional confusion: "Which doc version is final?" or "Has anyone updated the Trello card after that meeting?" She noticed colleagues frequently forgot to switch tasks in Trello or to notify the group if a file changed.

One afternoon, while exploring the "Apps" tab in Teams out of curiosity, Sarah saw a listing for Trello. A lightbulb went off: "Wait, we can show our Trello board *inside* Teams?" A few clicks later, she pinned it to her marketing channel as a new tab. Suddenly, her coworkers could see tasks right next to their daily conversation feed. Some were skeptical ("Another integration?"), but after a week, many realized they no longer had to keep multiple browser tabs open—Trello was just a quick channel click away.

Excited by this small success, Sarah browsed for other integrations. She found connectors that could alert the channel whenever a new lead form arrived, or a messaging extension letting them quickly poll each other about a design choice. She envisioned a day where the marketing team rarely left Teams to coordinate. Instead, they'd have a central place to talk, assign tasks, and share files. That dream aligned well with management's push for more synergy across Microsoft 365.

As Sarah discovered more potential apps—some from Microsoft, others from specialized vendors—she recognized that a bit of planning was needed. She didn't want random connectors spamming the channel with notifications. She also needed to check if these apps met 365 Strategies' security standards. Still, the possibilities excited her: by pulling the right tools into Teams, they'd streamline collaboration and cut down on the "Where's that link?" confusion that plagued so many projects.

Throughout the rest of this book, we'll follow Sarah's journey in harnessing the power of integrations to unify her team's workflow—without overwhelming them or risking data security. We'll show you how to implement best practices for governance, dig into Power Platform capabilities, and explore real-life automation scenarios that can save your colleagues hours of repetitive work. If you're ready to see how Teams evolves into your go-to workspace for everything from daily tasks to advanced data insights, buckle up—apps and integrations are about to make life simpler in ways you might not yet imagine.

CHAPTER 2: EXPLORING THE MICROSOFT TEAMS APP STORE

A big part of Teams' appeal is how easily you can add new apps to boost productivity. Instead of juggling multiple browser tabs or separate logins for every tool, you embed them directly in your team's workspace. But with hundreds of apps listed in the Microsoft Teams App Store, how do you decide which to install? And how can you be sure they're safe, or that your coworkers won't feel overwhelmed? In this chapter, we'll explore how to navigate the app catalog, highlight popular apps that frequently show up in successful Teams deployments, and share tips on rolling out new integrations so your teammates adopt them without confusion. Finally, we'll see how Sarah experiments with a polling app to liven up her marketing channel.

Much like a smartphone's app store, the Microsoft Teams App Store gives you one-stop access to an ecosystem of tools that can transform a basic chat app into a full-blown collaboration platform. Whether you need a project board, a polling widget, or a connector that automatically updates your channel whenever a new lead comes in, there's likely an integration for it. But with so many choices, it's useful to know how to search effectively, gauge permission requirements, and pick apps that genuinely enhance your workflow rather than clutter it. Let's start by learning how to navigate the app catalog in Teams.

When you open Teams, you'll notice an "Apps" icon (usually near the bottom of the left sidebar on desktop or the "More" section on mobile). Clicking that opens the Teams App Store, which sorts apps by categories like Productivity, Project Management, Education, Finance, and more. You can also use the search bar at the top if you already have an idea, like "Trello" or "Polly." Some apps highlight their "Top picks" or "Most popular," which can be a good starting point if you just want to see what's trending.

Once you select a category, the store shows you a grid of apps, each with a short description and star rating. Clicking an app reveals more details—screenshots, features, and any security or compliance notes. The "Add" or "Install" button places the app in your Teams environment, although your organization might require admin approval first. It's wise to read the permissions an app requests so you're not caught off guard if it wants to post messages in channels, read user data, or connect to external services.

When you add an app, you might see a consent prompt if it requires certain capabilities—like the ability to read channel messages or create tasks on your behalf. For smaller organizations, each user with certain privileges might be able to install apps. In larger companies, admin consent might be mandatory so that you don't inadvertently install an app that could compromise data.

If you see a message stating "An admin must approve this app," it means your company has set up governance rules to control the environment. You can usually request approval by sending an automated note to your IT or platform admin. They'll review the app's trust rating, check compliance notes, and decide whether to allow it globally or just for you. Once approved, the app becomes available in your tenant, so other colleagues might install it too, or your admin might limit it to a specific team if that's more appropriate.

While the App Store is huge, some integrations stand out as particularly useful across many departments:

1. Microsoft Planner: A first-party app from Microsoft that's ideal for task management in a Trello-like board format. You can create a Planner tab in a channel, letting your team see tasks, deadlines, and progress at a glance.

2. Trello: If your company already uses Trello for project boards, connecting it to Teams can keep tasks visible in the channel.

Coworkers can drag cards, assign tasks, or comment without leaving Teams.

3. Polly: A popular polling solution that helps you gather quick feedback—like picking meeting times, rating design options, or voting on lunch choices. You can launch polls directly in a channel or chat, and results show up in real time.

4. Microsoft Forms: Another poll or survey app, but it's also good for quiz-style forms or collecting longer answers. Great for quick questionnaires or check-ins.

5. OneNote: Though integrated by default in many ways, you can explicitly pin a OneNote notebook to a channel for brainstorming or note-taking.

6. Power BI: If your department uses BI dashboards, embedding them in Teams tabs can keep important metrics front and center.

Many third-party apps also cater to industry-specific needs, like a patient-record system for healthcare or a compliance system for finance. In most cases, you'll want to do a short pilot to see if the app's features truly benefit your workflows. If your team barely uses polls, installing multiple polling tools might just create noise.

Healthcare might see apps integrating with patient record management (like certain EHR or HIPAA-compliant systems). Finance might install connectors that post daily stock updates or currency exchange rates into a relevant channel. Tech companies often connect bug-tracking software (like Jira) so that every new issue logs a short note in their development channel. If you're in a specialized field, search the store for relevant keywords, or see if your vendor has created a Teams connector or bot. If not, you might consider building a custom integration yourself—something we'll address in later chapters.

One common pitfall is installing a bunch of apps and flooding channels with notifications. Users can quickly become fatigued by endless pings. Instead, aim for a purposeful approach:

1. Start small: Deploy an app that clearly solves a known problem. For example, if your daily stand-ups are messy, use a poll app (like Polly) to collect status updates asynchronously. Or if you have a big backlog of tasks, embed Planner in a project channel.

2. Test with a pilot: Recruit a few enthusiastic team members who are open to testing the app. Gather their feedback, refine settings, then present the success story to the wider group. This fosters acceptance because people see real benefits.

3. Gradual rollout: Not everyone needs every app. If an app is relevant only to marketing, you can limit it to the marketing team's channel. That keeps other areas from feeling spammed by irrelevant tools.

Remember, each app can post updates in your channels if you enable that. You might want to tweak the default notifications so the channel doesn't get overshadowed by bot messages. Disabling or restricting some notifications can maintain a clean feed, letting the app remain useful rather than annoying.

Even if an app is fairly intuitive, a short orientation helps. You might post a channel message or pinned note explaining how to interact with the new tool. For instance, if you install a connector that alerts the channel whenever a new sales lead is captured, clarify how to respond: "When you see a new lead posted, tag the relevant salesperson so they can follow up." Or if you add a Trello tab, walk teammates through how to open it and move cards around. Provide a quick bullet list or video link showing these actions.

If your organization is large, consider drafting basic tutorials or short "app introduction" sessions. The more comfortable employees feel, the less likely they'll resist or ignore the new integration. Encouraging questions and feedback can also surface potential misconfigurations before they cause real problems.

Bringing a Polling App (Polly) Into the Marketing Team

At 365 Strategies, Sarah noticed her marketing group often took quick votes on slogans or campaign angles. Typically, they'd do so via chat messages: "Which design do you like? Type yes/no!" But answers got lost in threads. She decided to install Polly, a well-known polling app, to formalize that process.

First, she opened the Teams App Store from the left sidebar, typed "Polly," and saw it listed with favorable reviews. The app asked for certain permissions, mainly to post poll results in channels and manage its bot messages. Since her admin settings allowed user consent for recognized apps, Sarah clicked "Install." Once installed, Polly appeared in her "Apps" sidebar, and she pinned it to the Marketing channel as a possible extension.

Before announcing it, Sarah tested a poll in a private chat with herself. She typed "@Polly create poll" and followed the prompts to name the question: "Which draft slogan is best?" She included three choices. Polly responded with a poll link, but in a real channel scenario, it would appear for everyone to click. Satisfied, Sarah posted a short message in the marketing channel: "We now have a polling app called Polly—type '@Polly create poll' to gather votes. Here's a quick tutorial." She attached a screenshot of her steps.

Later that week, when the team debated a new product name, Sarah posted an official poll using Polly. The results appeared in real time, with a small bar chart. Everyone found it more structured than random text replies, and no one missed the days of tallying "yes/no" messages manually. Encouraged, a coworker tried adding a short poll about the upcoming holiday schedule. The marketing channel's feed became more interactive without feeling spammy.

Seeing the success, Sarah reflected on how a single app bridged a small but annoying gap. People no longer had to guess how many "votes" each suggestion got; it was all in one neat poll. She realized that the real power of the Teams App Store lay in these targeted solutions. By picking an app that solved a concrete need, she avoided overwhelming her colleagues with multiple new integrations at once—and that's likely why adoption soared.

Exploring the Microsoft Teams App Store can expand your collaboration possibilities, bridging popular tools directly into your channels. Whether you integrate Trello boards, add polling features with Polly or Forms, or enable advanced connectors for real-time updates, each app should address a genuine workflow challenge to be worth adopting. As we continue in this book, we'll see how to manage app governance, harness the Power Platform for custom solutions, and handle more intricate scenarios like automation and custom bots. By following Sarah's lead—testing carefully, introducing one new integration at a time, and showing your team the direct benefits—you'll keep your Teams environment both robust and user-friendly.

CHAPTER 3: BUILT-IN APPS AND CUSTOMIZATION

Microsoft Teams shines not only because it supports countless external integrations, but also because it neatly embeds the Microsoft 365 suite—like OneNote, Excel, or Power BI—inside each channel. Instead of constantly opening separate Office apps or hunting down links, you can keep essential documents and dashboards front and center. By customizing each channel with tabs for spreadsheets, notes, or real-time analytics, your team stays aligned without flipping between a dozen different services. In this chapter, we'll explore how to leverage Microsoft's own apps in Teams, how to customize tabs and message extensions, and how to embed dynamic reports for data-driven decisions. Finally, we'll see how Sarah pins a live dashboard and spreadsheets in her project channel to reduce back-and-forth and centralize critical info.

While third-party integrations get a lot of buzz, many organizations rely heavily on Word, Excel, PowerPoint, OneNote, SharePoint, and other Microsoft 365 applications. Having these tools within Teams offers a consistent experience—no more emailing Excel files or storing them on multiple drives. Instead, you can pin relevant documents at the top of a channel, so team members click once to see the latest version and collaborate in real time. Microsoft also offers smaller features, like message extensions, that let you quickly reference files or create tasks in conversation. By blending these built-in apps with Teams' chat and meeting capabilities, you lay the groundwork for a more efficient workflow.

OneNote: If your team keeps a notebook of brainstorming ideas, meeting notes, or standard operating procedures, OneNote can live inside Teams as a dedicated tab. This eliminates scattered documents or sticky notes—everyone sees the same notebook pages, can type in real time, and find info quickly thanks to OneNote's search function. For instance, your marketing channel might have a "Campaign Ideas" OneNote tab for brainstorming slogans, while your finance channel might store budgeting policies in a separate notebook.

Lists: Microsoft Lists is a more recent addition, letting you track items in a table or board-like format directly in Teams. You can manage tasks, assets, or any custom data fields. For smaller teams, Lists might serve as an alternative to more complex project management tools. By pinning a Lists tab, your channel members can add, edit, or filter entries without leaving Teams, and you can set rules or alerts for when certain changes occur.

PowerPoint and Excel: If you're presenting slides often, a PowerPoint stored in SharePoint can be pinned at the top of a channel. Teammates can open it in Teams, co-author slides, or even start an impromptu meeting to walk through changes. Similarly, an Excel file used for tracking project budgets or timelines can become a channel tab, ensuring everyone always references the most up-to-date version. No more emailing "Budget_v6_final.xlsx."

SharePoint Libraries: Each channel in Teams corresponds to a folder in a SharePoint document library. You can highlight that library as a tab or embed a specific subfolder, letting members quickly browse or upload files. This simplifies file organization—people click the tab and see a structured view rather than hunting through the "Files" tab or separate SharePoint site.

When a document is crucial to a project—like a main project plan or a shared campaign outline—pinning it as a tab at the top of the channel saves time. Anyone can open the channel, click the tab, and start editing. It also reduces the risk of multiple, conflicting versions. Just note that you should keep tab usage purposeful: if you add too many tabs, people might not notice them all. Focus on the real "hero documents" that the team checks daily or weekly. Occasionally rotate or update tabs if certain files become outdated.

Each channel or private group chat has a "+" button near the top, letting you add a new tab. You might choose a Microsoft 365 app (like OneNote or Excel) or a popular third-party integration (like Trello). The idea is to keep the channel aligned with its purpose. If you're running a product launch, you might pin a "Launch Timeline" Excel doc and a "Marketing Plan" PowerPoint. If it's a helpdesk channel, you might pin a SharePoint-based FAQ. By customizing each channel's tabs, you shape the user experience so that relevant info is just a click away.

Group chats—like a chat with four marketing members—also support tabs, though many teams underutilize this. If a small working group constantly references a particular file, why not pin it in the chat? That way, it's always accessible, even if the chat moves on to new topics. Just remember that ephemeral group chats might eventually get deleted or archived. If it's a longer-term project, a channel might be better.

Messaging extensions let you access an app's functionality right in the conversation. For example, the Power Automate extension could let you trigger a workflow from the message box. Or the Praise extension can instantly send kudos to a coworker. If you have a particular action you do often—like searching a knowledge base or injecting a snippet from a library—check if there's a messaging extension that shortens the step. Instead of toggling to another window, you can type a keyword and select an item that appears inline.

Also, pinned chat shortcuts might appear in the message composer as small icons, so if you're frequently polling the group with an app like Polly, you can click its icon to craft a new poll without leaving the chat. Overusing message extensions can clutter the interface, though, so pick carefully which ones to pin. If your channels turn into a flurry of extension-based posts, your team might miss important discussions.

For teams that live on data—like sales, finance, or operations—Power BI integration can be a game-changer. If you have a Power BI workspace with important dashboards (like sales performance, budget tracking, or supply chain metrics), you can embed a specific report tab in your Teams channel. Users see real-time data without opening the separate Power BI site. They can filter, drill down on charts, or share snapshots with the channel. This approach fosters a data-driven culture, letting everyone keep an eye on metrics and quickly discuss anomalies or trends in the same space.

Some organizations even schedule a recurring channel discussion—like "Monthly Metrics Review"—and encourage participants to open the Power BI tab, exploring the data in sync. It's effectively a digital "war room" for analyzing stats and making decisions, minus the overhead of traditional slides or separate logins.

When you pin a Power BI report or embed a SharePoint folder, the users must already have permission to view that content. If an external guest or someone outside that group tries to open the tab, they'll see an error or a request for access. Often, adopting a simpler, role-based permission model in Microsoft 365 helps ensure that if someone belongs to a certain channel, they also have the correct file or report privileges. If you're dealing with sensitive data (like finance or HR info), double-check your sharing settings to avoid accidental exposure. Label tabs clearly— especially if some are confidential—and consider restricting the channel membership to only those who truly need it.

Pinning Spreadsheets and a Live Dashboard in One Place

At 365 Strategies, Sarah's project team for a new product launch had been jumping between an Excel sheet for the timeline, a separate SharePoint doc for budget notes, and a third platform for analytics on user engagement. Each conversation in Teams ended with someone saying, "Hang on, let me open the spreadsheet," or "I'll get that data from the analytics dashboard and paste a screenshot here." It was time-consuming, and data sometimes got stale.

So, Sarah added two new tabs in their "Product Launch" channel: one for the "Launch_Timeline.xlsx" file, which lived in SharePoint, and another for the "UserEngagement" Power BI dashboard. Now, whenever someone asked, "What's our current milestone?" they could click the "Timeline" tab and see the latest Excel data. And if the conversation turned to how many users were testing the beta version, they could open the "UserEngagement" tab and see real-time charts.

Sarah also found that her colleagues appreciated that they didn't have to memorize which link or folder the Excel sheet was in—nor request a fresh link from the marketing lead. Everything was pinned in the channel's top bar. The group even discovered they could open the spreadsheet right in Teams, editing simultaneously. A few folks jumped into the Power BI tab after hours to explore user feedback stats, posting screenshots in the channel for next morning's discussion. The result? Fewer "Let me dig up that link" moments, more direct collaboration, and faster decisions.

Seeing how well it worked, Sarah shared a short post: "If your doc or data is crucial to the project, consider pinning it as a tab. Saves everyone a few clicks—and reduces the chance we're referencing old files." The positive responses reaffirmed that small customizations go a long way to unify teamwork under one digital roof.

Microsoft Teams isn't just about external apps. Its tight integration with core Microsoft 365 tools can transform a channel into a central repository for crucial files, notes, and data insights. By adding OneNote, Excel, Power BI dashboards, or SharePoint libraries as tabs, you let people interact with essential info on the fly—reducing back-and-forth and version confusion. Messaging extensions further cut down on context switches, making frequent actions accessible right in the conversation box.

As you build familiarity with these built-in apps, remember to keep it purposeful: not every file needs a pinned tab, and not every extension needs to be installed. Balance is key. In the upcoming chapters, we'll delve into how to manage apps at scale—governance policies, security considerations, and tips for using the Power Platform to build your own custom solutions. With a thoughtful approach, you'll empower your team to do more directly in Teams, turning each channel into a living workspace where documents, dashboards, and discussions coexist seamlessly.

CHAPTER 4: DEEP DIVE INTO THE POWER PLATFORM

Microsoft Teams is already a potent hub for chatting, video calls, and embedded apps—but there's a whole other layer of potential lying just below the surface: the Power Platform. Composed of tools like Power Automate, Power Apps, Power Virtual Agents, and Power BI, this suite can transform Teams from a simple collaboration tool into a launchpad for custom workflows, data insights, and interactive bots. By combining these low-code (and sometimes no-code) solutions with Teams, even non-developers can streamline repetitive tasks, gather real-time analytics, and automate common processes. In this chapter, we'll explore the core Power Platform products, how they integrate with Teams, and what you need to begin building or administering these solutions. Finally, we'll follow Sarah as she discovers how the Power Platform can free her coworkers from mundane chores, unleashing creativity and collaboration in new ways.

Modern businesses often juggle specialized software, spreadsheets, or homegrown systems for everyday tasks—like logging approvals, updating inventory, or collecting feedback. The Power Platform centralizes these tasks by letting you create or connect apps without heavy coding. Essentially, it democratizes application development, so employees who know the business processes best can design the solutions, rather than waiting for IT to code from scratch.

1. Power Automate (formerly Flow): A tool for creating automated workflows that link different apps or services. You might use Power Automate to trigger actions, like sending an email or updating a database, when someone posts a certain message in a Teams channel or when a new row appears in an Excel file.

2. Power Apps: A platform to build custom apps—often for mobile or web—that tap into data sources such as SharePoint, Excel, SQL databases, or other connectors. These apps can gather data from employees or display data in a simplified interface, all without needing advanced programming.

3. Power Virtual Agents: A tool for creating chatbots that can answer questions, guide users through processes, or escalate queries to human agents. In Teams, you can deploy these bots to handle FAQs or route calls to the right department.

4. Power BI: We've touched on Power BI in prior chapters, but it's part of the Power Platform as well. It helps visualize data from multiple sources, and embedded dashboards can appear in Teams channels or personal apps, showing real-time analytics.

By tapping into the Power Platform within Teams, you turn everyday channels into dynamic workflows. Instead of manually tracking approvals or emailing an external system, you might build a Power App embedded in a channel tab, letting colleagues submit requests or update statuses. If you prefer automation, Power Automate can watch for a trigger (like a new message with a specific keyword) and then run a workflow—perhaps creating a Planner task or sending a summary email. The ultimate goal is reducing friction: employees already live in Teams for messaging, so why not let them do much of their process work there too?

Let's imagine a scenario: your HR department wants to simplify onboarding. Today, each new hire receives a flurry of emails, and various managers must approve accounts or send them documents. With Power Automate, you could create a flow that triggers when HR enters a new hire in a SharePoint list—automatically generating tasks in Planner for the IT department to set up equipment, emailing a welcome packet, and posting a "Welcome!" message in a Teams channel. If certain conditions arise (like the hire's location requiring additional paperwork), the flow might notify the relevant local manager.

Meanwhile, you might have built a Power App that tracks each new hire's progress. By adding that app as a tab in the HR channel, team members can update statuses, see who completed orientation, and escalate issues. If employees have frequent questions about benefits or the process, a Power Virtual Agent could handle basic Q&A, offering quick links or forms. And if leadership wants a high-level snapshot of how many hires are in each stage, a Power BI dashboard pinned to the channel might visualize that data in real time.

This example shows how the tools can mesh: Automate manages background workflows, Apps handle user input, Virtual Agents handle queries, and BI handles reporting. All anchored inside a Teams workspace—so no more chasing spreadsheets or endless email threads.

- Tabs: You can pin a Power App or a Power BI dashboard as a channel tab, letting users interact directly.

- Bots: A Power Virtual Agent can appear as a Teams bot. People type questions, the bot replies with info or triggers further workflows.

- Connectors & Messaging Extensions: Some Power Automate flows can post updates to a Teams channel or create new tasks in a side panel. As your solution evolves, you might add a messaging extension that queries data from your Power App.

By layering these integration points, a single channel can become a mini control center for a whole process. For instance, your #HR-Onboarding channel might feature a pinned Power App, a bot pinned in the chat for quick Q&A, and an automated flow that posts a welcome message for each new hire.

The Power Platform is often described as low-code, meaning it's approachable for "citizen developers"—people who understand the business process well but aren't professional coders. They can use drag-and-drop interfaces, formula-like expressions (reminiscent of Excel), and pre-built templates. However, for more complex scenarios or custom connectors, you might need some IT or developer help—like writing advanced queries, building custom APIs, or ensuring robust security.

A typical enterprise approach is that business-side employees do initial prototypes in Power Apps or Power Automate, while IT oversees governance, sets up data gateways, or polishes the final product. This partnership can accelerate innovation, because the domain experts create the workflow logic, with minimal reliance on developers for every tweak.

Power Platform usage can require additional licensing depending on the complexity of the app or automation. For instance, if your flows connect to premium services (like certain SQL databases or advanced connectors), you might need a higher-tier license. Similarly, large-scale usage of Power Virtual Agents might require separate capacity. Check Microsoft's licensing docs or consult with your admin to confirm which plan covers your intended scenario.

Governance is also crucial. Without guardrails, employees might create dozens of random flows that spam channels or accidentally expose sensitive data. Many organizations set up an environment strategy—like a dedicated "Dev" environment for experimentation and a "Prod" environment for approved solutions. An admin center for Power Platform helps manage these solutions, assign owners, and ensure security compliance. Ideally, you'll define guidelines on naming flows, storing data, and who can share apps.

Discovering Power Platform's Potential for Automation

After seeing how a simple polling app (Polly) in Teams could save time, Sarah grew curious about other tools. One day, she attended an internal workshop titled "Empowering Teams with Power Platform," led by a Microsoft consultant. The presenter showed how Power Automate could watch for a new record in a "Client Requests" SharePoint list, then automatically create a Teams post in the Sales channel tagging the relevant rep. Another example featured a custom Power App that let employees submit a marketing asset request, which automatically triggered an approval workflow. Sarah was amazed that these solutions required little coding—mostly a drag-and-drop interface and some logic expressions.

During the workshop, participants built a quick flow: if someone posted a file named "Invoice" in the Finance channel, the system added a row in an Excel tracker. Sarah realized she could adapt this idea for marketing files or design assets. She also saw a short demo of Power Virtual Agents, where a "HelpBot" answered HR FAQs. She typed a sample question, "How do I request vacation days?" and the bot responded with the correct procedure, even linking to the request form.

Intrigued, Sarah thought of her marketing team's repeated tasks—like adding new campaign data to an Excel file, emailing a summary, and messaging colleagues. She pictured a flow that could do half those steps automatically. The consultant emphasized that citizen developers— people like Sarah, who understand the workflow but aren't full-time programmers—could build such flows with guidance from a central admin team. That day, Sarah walked away confident that these low-code solutions could significantly cut down her team's routine busywork.

Shortly afterward, she scheduled a brainstorm meeting with one of the consultants and her department lead. Her pitch: let's identify three repetitive tasks that eat time and see if we can build mini apps or flows to handle them. "We don't need anything super fancy," she told them, "just enough to see what's possible—maybe a form for requesting design help, or a flow that notifies our channel whenever a new sponsor signs up." The manager agreed to let her pilot these ideas, provided IT gave a green light. Sarah felt energized: if a simple polling app had boosted engagement, imagine how a well-built Power App could transform their entire marketing workflow.

The Power Platform fundamentally expands Microsoft Teams from a collaboration tool into a versatile framework for automation, custom apps, bots, and data insights. Power Automate handles workflow automation, Power Apps offers user-friendly app-building, Power Virtual

Agents powers chatbots, and Power BI provides rich analytics. By leveraging these tools within Teams, everyday users and non-technical staff (the "citizen developers") can create tailored solutions that reduce manual tasks and unify data in a central hub.

Of course, successful rollouts require thoughtful governance—defining who can build or publish apps, how data is secured, and what licensing is needed. Training is also key: employees who grasp the basics of flows or app building can innovate on their own, but they'll need some orientation to avoid pitfalls. In the upcoming chapters, we'll dive deeper into how to manage these apps in Teams, ensure compliance, and share real-world examples of how automation can save hours of grunt work. Following Sarah's lead, you'll see how even small Power Platform pilots can spark big leaps in productivity.

CHAPTER 5: AUTOMATING WORKFLOWS WITH POWER AUTOMATE

One of the biggest game-changers in modern collaboration is cutting down the busywork—those small but time-consuming tasks like sending routine updates, gathering approvals, or updating trackers after a meeting. Power Automate (formerly known as Flow) is Microsoft's answer to these challenges, letting you build simple or sophisticated workflows across different apps—including Microsoft Teams, SharePoint, Outlook, and even third-party services. This chapter delves into how Power Automate works, how you can create flows that integrate with Teams, and real-world scenarios where automation frees you and your colleagues from tedious manual chores. Finally, we'll see how Sarah automates her team's marketing collateral approvals, marveling at the significant drop in email back-and-forth.

Modern tools like Teams bring people together, but many repetitive tasks still lurk—like emailing the same update after each meeting, or pinging certain teammates whenever a new file is added to a channel. These small tasks are ripe for automation. By letting a well-designed flow handle them, you reduce human error and free up time for more meaningful work. Power Automate is built for exactly this: it's low-code, approachable by non-developers, and seamlessly integrates with Microsoft 365 services (plus many external apps). Let's see the core mechanics before diving into practical use cases.

At its core, every flow in Power Automate has three main ingredients:

1. Trigger: The event that sets the flow in motion—like "a new file is uploaded in a SharePoint folder," or "a new message is posted in the #Marketing channel," or "it's 8:00 AM every Monday."

2. Actions: The steps the flow takes after the trigger fires. For example, "Send a Teams message to the #Marketing channel," or "Create a record in Excel," or "Notify me via email." You can stack multiple actions in sequence, passing data from step to step.

3. Connectors: These are pre-built links to hundreds of apps and services—like Teams, Outlook, SharePoint, Trello, Salesforce, etc. Connectors let your flow talk to these systems, retrieving or sending data without you having to code the integration.

Imagine a flow triggered whenever a user posts a message in the #Requests channel containing the word "urgent." The next action might be "Send a chat message to the manager," or "Create a new Planner task labeled urgent." All it takes is configuring the right trigger, picking actions, and mapping fields or content. No advanced coding necessary— just pick from dropdowns or use a visual logic builder.

Power Automate offers templates—pre-built flows for common scenarios. You might see templates like "Post a message to Teams when a file is added to OneDrive," or "Get approval for new items in a SharePoint list." These templates jumpstart your flow creation. You select one, connect your accounts, tweak a few details, and you're done.

If no template matches your needs, you can create a flow from scratch, adding a trigger, then stepwise actions. Though it's more work, you gain full control—like adding conditional logic ("If the file is in the Finance folder, notify the finance group; otherwise, notify marketing."). As you grow comfortable, you'll find you can chain multiple steps, filter data, or even loop over items in a list, building fairly sophisticated automations.

Since Teams is a hub for daily discussion, hooking it into Power Automate can keep everyone informed without manual updates. Common examples:

1. New File Notifications: Suppose you have a "Client Assets" channel. You can build a flow: *Trigger:* When a file is uploaded to the "ClientAssets" folder in SharePoint. *Action:* Post a message to

the #ClientAssets channel with the file name and link. Now nobody misses new uploads.

2. Mentions to Specific Users: If a certain keyword appears in your channel, a flow might mention the relevant user or group. For instance, "If someone types '@helpdesk' in the #ITSupport channel, send an alert to the helpdesk manager."

3. Daily Summaries: Some teams want a daily recap at 9 AM—like how many tasks were completed or how many leads were generated. Power Automate can pull data from Excel or a CRM and post a short message each morning in Teams. No human needs to do that manual report anymore.

Each scenario uses a Teams-related trigger or action. For instance, a "New message in channel" trigger can parse the text. The "Post a message (V3)" action can place a summary in a different channel or mention a user. By carefully layering these triggers and actions, you create a dynamic system that keeps the right people informed at the right time.

Teams approvals can lighten the load of emailing back and forth. Power Automate includes an "Approval" action, letting you define who must approve, how many approvals are needed, and what happens on acceptance or rejection. For instance:

- Vacation Requests: Employee fills out a quick Teams form or posts in #VacationRequests. A flow triggers, sending an approval notification to the manager. They click "Approve" or "Reject," possibly with a comment. If approved, the flow might auto-update a vacation calendar in SharePoint.

- Document Sign-Off: For marketing collaterals, you can do the same. Once someone uploads a final PDF or design, the flow prompts the brand manager for sign-off. If the brand manager clicks "Approve," an "All Approved!" message appears in the channel, and the file moves from a "Draft" folder to "Approved" folder.

These streamlined approvals help teams avoid "Who's signed off yet?" confusion. Everyone sees the approval status in a single place, and the chat or channel can log the final outcome.

Maybe your department holds a weekly project review. Typically, you'd gather numbers from a few sources, compile them into a short summary, and paste it in the #ProjectUpdates channel. With Power Automate, you might create a scheduled flow for every Friday at 4 PM. It pulls data from an Excel file or SharePoint list (like "Tasks completed this week," "Pending tasks," etc.), formats a short message, and posts it to #ProjectUpdates. Now, you'll never forget to send that weekly status, and it's always updated from the source data. You can still add personal remarks if needed, but the base info arrives automatically.

Thanks to the wide array of connectors in Power Automate, you can integrate non-Microsoft apps, too. If you have a CRM like Salesforce or a marketing platform like Mailchimp, a flow might watch for "new lead created" or "campaign updated" events. When triggered, it posts a message in Teams, giving your channel real-time insights. Or if your finance team uses a separate billing system, you could build a flow to note each new invoice in a dedicated channel, letting account managers quickly see new charges without logging into that billing system.

These cross-platform workflows elevate Teams from "where we chat" to "where data meets conversations." People can comment right under the posted info, tagging colleagues or clarifying next steps. Combined with a Teams-based approval or mention system, these flows make your entire organization more responsive.

Automating Marketing Collateral Reviews
At 365 Strategies, Sarah's marketing department frequently created brochures, social media graphics, or ad copy. Each piece typically needed review by multiple managers, and an email thread sometimes got lost. Each manager might say "Approved" or "Needs changes," leading to more emails. Sarah realized Power Automate could simplify this.

She built a flow: *Trigger:* When a file is added to the "CollateralDrafts" folder in SharePoint. *Action 1:* Create an Approval request assigned to the brand manager and creative director. *Action 2:* Notify the #Marketing channel that a new file awaits review. *Action 3 (on Approve):* Move the file to "CollateralApproved" folder, then post a success message ("File X has been approved!"). *Action 4 (on Reject):* Post a note with the reviewer's comments in the channel, prompting the designer to revise.

After some trial and error (like making sure the flow recognized which file was attached), Sarah tested it with a small design. The brand manager got an approval prompt in Teams, clicked Approve, typed "Looks great!" and the system automatically moved the file. The #Marketing channel displayed a neat "Approved" message. No email thread or external steps needed. Everyone saw the final result, and the designer immediately knew they could finalize the campaign materials.

Within a week, several team members noticed fewer "FYI, please review" emails. Instead, new drafts triggered a flow in the background, capturing approvals right in Teams. The brand manager praised Sarah: "This saved me from rummaging through my inbox for attachments. Everything's in the channel, with a clear Accept/Reject interface." Sarah realized how a seemingly small automation cut down the friction around design reviews, letting colleagues focus on creativity rather than bureaucracy. She started brainstorming other mundane tasks they could automate—like daily analytics updates or scheduling reminders.

Power Automate is a cornerstone of the Power Platform, giving you the ability to orchestrate tasks and data flows across Teams and beyond. By setting up triggers, actions, and connectors, you can automate notifications, approvals, and routine updates—freeing employees from repetitive chores. Once you dip your toes in, you'll see how a single well-placed flow can reduce confusion and unify your collaborative processes inside Teams.

As you continue exploring, keep an eye on the user experience: ensure the flows don't spam channels, confirm they handle edge cases (like multiple reviewers or large attachments), and remain transparent to the team. In upcoming chapters, we'll expand on how to manage these solutions at scale—covering governance, advanced data handling, and custom bots. For now, let Sarah's success inspire you: small automations can reap big dividends, fueling a culture where people rely on Teams not just for chatter, but as a genuine engine of productivity.

CHAPTER 6: BUILDING CUSTOM APPS WITH POWER APPS

When everyday tools don't quite meet your team's needs, Power Apps comes to the rescue. Designed for "citizen developers" and professional coders alike, Power Apps allows you to build tailored applications—forms, dashboards, data-entry tools—that can run on desktops or mobile devices. By embedding these apps in Microsoft Teams, you can weave custom functionality directly into your collaboration spaces, letting coworkers quickly access or update data without bouncing between separate sites. In this chapter, we'll look at how Power Apps works, explain the difference between canvas apps and model-driven apps, show you how to embed them in Teams, and discuss security measures. Then we'll follow Sarah as she builds a simple contact directory for her department, revealing how even non-developers can create user-friendly solutions in just a few steps.

While Teams offers many pre-built integrations, every organization has unique workflows or data sets that might not match an off-the-shelf app. Perhaps you need a form to log client interactions, a custom dashboard to track internal requests, or a simple mobile tool for employees on the go. Power Apps helps fill these gaps with minimal coding, thanks to its drag-and-drop interface, formula-based logic, and ready-made templates.

Microsoft splits Power Apps into two main types—canvas apps for highly customized designs and model-driven apps for more data-centric solutions. Understanding these approaches helps you decide which route to take, especially if you plan to embed the app in Teams for your entire department or company to use.

- Canvas Apps: Think of these like a blank canvas where you place buttons, text boxes, and galleries wherever you want. You control the layout and look, and you can connect data sources such as SharePoint, Excel, SQL, or other connectors. Canvas apps feel very visual: you drag components onto a screen, set properties, and write formula-like expressions (similar to Excel) to handle logic. This style is great for mobile-friendly solutions or when you need a unique interface.

- Model-Driven Apps: Instead of designing every button from scratch, you define data in the Microsoft Dataverse (a built-in data platform) and let Power Apps generate views and forms automatically. These apps follow a structured approach, focusing on relationships between data tables. You can still tweak the layout and logic, but model-driven apps emphasize data consistency and quick creation of form-based solutions. They often suit scenarios where you want to manage records in a more standardized UI, and less about custom visuals.

Which one you choose depends on your scenario. If you want a highly customized layout—like a tablet-friendly form that sales reps fill out—canvas might be best. If you have a large dataset in Dataverse and prefer a dynamic, data-driven interface, model-driven might be the way. For many Teams integrations, canvas apps are popular because they can embed seamlessly and look appealing to users accustomed to basic forms.

When creating a canvas app, you'll open Power Apps Studio, which provides a drag-and-drop environment. On the left, you see a tree view of screens and controls; on the right, you have properties for whichever control is selected. At the top, you'll find a formula bar reminiscent of Excel, where you can type expressions like If(IsSelected, "blue", "gray") or Patch(MyDataSource, {ID: ThisItem.ID, Status: "Approved"}).

For model-driven apps, the interface is more about defining tables (entities), relationships, and forms. You pick which columns appear in a view, how records are laid out, and the basic navigation. Then Power Apps Studio auto-generates the main app structure, which you can refine with components like charts or dashboards.

Once you've built an app in Power Apps, you can integrate it into Teams in a few steps:

1. Publish Your App: Make sure it's saved and shared with the relevant people. If it's a canvas app, you might set the environment to a certain security group or default environment.

2. Open Teams: Go to the channel or chat where you want the app available.

3. Add a Tab: Click the "+" button at the top of the channel, find "Power Apps," and select the app you want to embed. If you don't see it, ensure you're in the right environment or have the right permissions.

4. Name the Tab: Give it a descriptive label like "Contact Directory" or "Vacation Requests."

Now your custom solution appears as a tab alongside "Posts" and "Files." Users click it, see your app's screen, and can interact with data, fill forms, or run queries. Because it lives inside Teams, they don't need a separate login (provided your environment is configured), and they stay focused on the workspace they use daily.

Beyond pinning it to one channel, you might want broader reach—for example, letting all employees access a company-wide app. You can distribute your Power App via the Teams App Store if you package it as a custom Teams application. This involves creating an app manifest that points to your Power App, setting icons and descriptions, and deciding who can install it. Alternatively, you can simply share the app link via your internal portal or intranet.

However, keep in mind licensing: some advanced Power Apps require premium connectors or Dataverse usage, which might cost extra. Check your existing Microsoft 365 plan to see if these features are included. Also consider support—if the app is for a small team, you might handle user questions informally. If it's for the entire company, plan for a help channel or short training sessions so employees know how to navigate it.

When your app interacts with sensitive data—like HR records or customer info—you need robust governance. Power Apps uses environments to keep different solutions separated. For instance, you might have a "Dev" environment for testing new apps and a "Prod" environment for stable ones. Admins can define Data Loss Prevention (DLP) policies that dictate which connectors can interact—for example, you might block mixing personal connectors (like a user's Dropbox) with corporate data sources (like SharePoint) to prevent leaks.

User roles also matter. A "Maker" can build or modify an app, while a "User" only runs it. If your app writes data to SharePoint or Dataverse, ensure the correct permissions are in place so employees see only what they're allowed. This can mean row-level security for model-driven apps or item-level security in SharePoint. The better your planning, the safer your data remains.

It's tempting to share a new Power App widely so everyone can benefit. But if the app handles confidential records, you must confirm each viewer is authorized. For instance, if you made a "Performance Reviews" app, only managers and HR might have read/write access to those records. If you embed that app in a public channel, it might inadvertently reveal data to all members, violating privacy rules.

One approach is to place the app in a private channel restricted to certain user roles. Another is to rely on the underlying data source's security. For instance, if the app pulls from a secure SharePoint list that only HR can read, anyone else sees an empty screen or error. In any case, regularly audit your environment—over time, staff changes might alter who should see what.

Prototyping a Simple Contact Directory

At 365 Strategies, Sarah's marketing department complained that they had no quick reference for colleagues in other departments—like who's in finance, what's the official phone extension, who's the right contact for purchase orders, etc. Sarah recalled a workshop on Power Apps, so she decided to build a "Contact Directory" canvas app.

She started by creating a SharePoint list with columns: Name, Department, Role, Email, Extension. Then in Power Apps Studio, she picked "Create an app from data," selecting that SharePoint list. The studio auto-generated a canvas with a gallery screen (listing all contacts) and a detail screen (showing the selected contact's info). She fine-tuned the layout, added a search box at the top, and adjusted fonts to match the company's branding. It took only a few hours of exploration and some quick how-to videos.

Once she was satisfied, she saved and shared the app with her marketing team. Next, she opened Teams, went to the #Marketing channel, clicked "+" to add a tab, chose "Power Apps," and found "Contact Directory." She pinned it, labeling the tab "Contact Directory." Immediately, her teammates saw a simple directory inside Teams, letting them search or tap a contact for more details.

When her peers opened the tab, they assumed it was some fancy external software. Sarah explained she built it with no advanced coding, just connecting a SharePoint list. People liked how they could quickly see each name and extension, saving them from rummaging through an outdated spreadsheet or the global address book. The brand manager asked if it could be extended to show a small photo or handle staff who changed roles. Sarah realized she could easily add a photo column in SharePoint and refresh the app layout, all within an afternoon.

Word spread that Sarah's app saved a lot of guesswork. The HR department inquired if something similar could display a "Who's On Vacation" board. Sarah saw how they could replicate the steps, hooking the app to a different SharePoint list. This success story signaled a new era for her company, where non-IT employees could craft quick solutions for daily needs, all embedded in the same Teams environment.

Building Power Apps for Teams merges the best of both worlds: easy low-code development with the central, collaborative environment of Teams. Whether you design a canvas app for flexible layouts or a model-driven app for structured data, you can embed it as a channel tab or even distribute it across the organization. Throughout the process, keep security and governance top of mind, ensuring only authorized users can access sensitive records.

As Sarah's story shows, you don't need to be a seasoned developer to create useful, user-friendly apps. Simple prototypes can solve real pain points, prompting further exploration of advanced features or additional data sources. Next, we'll dive into Power Virtual Agents—another Power Platform gem—highlighting how chatbots can handle FAQs, triage user queries, and seamlessly integrate with Teams channels. By adding apps and bots together, you'll empower your workforce to accomplish more right inside their everyday workspace, forging a robust ecosystem of custom collaboration tools.

CHAPTER 7: CONVERSATIONAL INTERFACES WITH POWER VIRTUAL AGENTS

Microsoft Teams can be much more than a place for text-based chats and pinned documents. With Power Virtual Agents, you can introduce intelligent chatbots right within your channels—bots that can answer FAQs, collect information, or connect users to deeper resources. Instead of staff repeatedly handling the same questions or manually routing user inquiries, bots can free up time by automating those tasks. In this chapter, we'll explore how to set up a Teams-based bot using Power Virtual Agents, touch on advanced capabilities like natural language understanding, and share best practices for ensuring a smooth user experience. Finally, we'll follow Sarah at 365 Strategies as she builds an HR FAQ bot that alleviates routine queries, giving the HR team more room for complex issues.

As employees rely on Teams for day-to-day collaboration, they naturally ask questions—about policies, procedures, or system statuses—in chat channels or direct messages. If these questions repeat often, it's inefficient for a human to answer them each time. Enter Power Virtual Agents (PVA): a low-code platform for creating conversational bots that handle everything from simple Q&A to branching dialogue and back-end data lookups. By embedding a bot in Teams, you turn repeated, mundane queries into an automated flow, letting staff quickly get answers without waiting for a human responder. Meanwhile, your teams can still escalate trickier queries to real people.

Power Virtual Agents offers a web-based designer for crafting "topics"—the conversation paths and responses your bot can handle.

After picking or creating a Microsoft Dataverse environment for your bot, you define how it should behave in Teams.

1. Create a Bot: In Power Virtual Agents, click "Create a bot," select your environment, and name it (e.g., "HRHelperBot").

2. Set Up Topics: Topics are triggers and dialogs. For instance, "Vacation Policy" might be a topic triggered by keywords like "vacation," "leave," or "time off." The conversation flow can greet the user, answer basic details, and optionally escalate if the question is more complex.

3. Configure Bot Channels: Once your bot logic is ready, you can add a "Teams channel." This publishes your bot into Microsoft Teams. Then you distribute it—like a standard Teams app or by sharing a link—to employees who may want to chat with it.

By default, PVA includes some sample topics (like a "Greeting" or "Escalation" scenario). You can modify or delete them, add custom triggers, and expand your dialogues with conditions or user input prompts. The interface is drag-and-drop, with branching paths where you define what the bot says next based on user responses.

A typical PVA topic looks like a flowchart:

- If the user's message matches certain keywords (like "benefits info"), the conversation jumps to that topic.

- You might greet them, display info, then ask if that answered their question.

- If not, you could prompt them for more details or escalate to a Teams channel or human agent.

You can also trigger actions in the middle of a conversation—like calling a Power Automate flow if the user wants to log a ticket or look up data in a CRM. This expands your bot's power from pure Q&A to interactive transactions. For instance, if an employee asks "What's my PTO balance?" the bot can run a flow that queries your HR system, then returns the result. This might require more advanced setup (like API connectors), but it's a game-changer for supporting employees without manual overhead.

Power Virtual Agents comes with a natural language understanding (NLU) engine that tries to parse user input beyond just exact keyword matches. For example, if your topic triggers on "vacation days," the user might type "How do I request time off?" and the bot can still route them to the correct topic if it's trained on synonyms or intent matching. You define synonyms or variations in your topic's trigger phrases. Over time, you can refine or add phrases whenever you notice the bot missing relevant queries.

If you want deeper NLU, you can tie your bot to LUIS (Language Understanding Intelligent Service) or the evolving AI models from Microsoft, but the built-in approach often suffices for common scenarios. The key is consistently training your bot with real user expressions, so it grows more accurate.

Beyond the standard Q&A, your bot might connect to:

- Dataverse tables: If you store data in Microsoft Dataverse, the bot can read or write records, like an internal employee directory or a helpdesk ticket system.

- Power Automate flows: A node in your conversation can call a flow that queries external APIs—like a weather service or your HR management system—then return the result to the user.

- Custom Connectors: If you have an internal API, you can create a custom connector, letting the bot securely access your unique data. This step often requires more advanced setup, but it can yield powerful results, such as retrieving an employee's pending tasks or listing open support tickets from a third-party system.

By hooking into these data sources, your bot transitions from a simple FAQ engine to an interactive agent capable of performing real actions—like capturing feedback, generating a PDF, or updating a SharePoint list.

The best chatbots solve well-defined problems. Employees often resent bots that spout generic marketing lines or direct them in circles. So, identify a repeated scenario—like HR frequently fielding "How do I reset my 401(k) password?" or "Where can I see my pay stubs?"—and build topics covering these. Or if your support team gets the same "How do I connect to the VPN?" question dozens of times, a bot can guide them step by step. This clarity ensures your bot doesn't try to be everything at once.

If you want the bot to escalate certain issues to a real human, plan that path in the conversation. Maybe the user says "This didn't help," so the bot can @mention a relevant channel or create a ticket. Communicate that your bot is a first-level resource, not a full replacement for human judgment, so users know they can still get personal help when needed.

While some employees might intuitively chat with the bot, others may not know it exists or how to phrase questions. A short training or pinned message in your channel helps. "Want quick answers to HR policies? Type '@HRHelperBot vacation' to see how many days you have left." Encouraging specific keywords or showing sample queries can reduce frustration. Over time, you can analyze transcripts or usage logs to see which phrases users type, then add or refine topics to improve coverage.

Also, watch out for the "novelty factor." In early days, some employees might test the bot with off-topic or joke questions. That's okay—just ensure your bot politely handles "I don't understand" scenarios, or it might appear broken. As people see actual value—like instantly retrieving info they used to email HR for—the novelty becomes genuine adoption.

Building an HR FAQ Bot for Common Questions

At 365 Strategies, the HR department kept fielding repetitive queries: "How many vacation days do I have left?" "What's the maternity leave policy?" "Where's the form for changing my health plan?" The HR manager confided in Sarah, saying they'd love a self-service solution so staff could find answers without emailing or pinging HR individually. Sarah suggested creating a chatbot with Power Virtual Agents.

She started by listing frequently asked questions, noting keywords like "vacation," "maternity," "benefits," "address change," etc. In the PVA interface, she created a new bot named "HRHelperBot," then added a topic called "Vacation FAQ." Under "Trigger Phrases," she included "vacation," "leave," "time off," "PTO." The conversation flow explained how many days employees typically receive, plus instructions for requesting them in the HR system. If an employee typed "I'm not sure about my days," the bot explained they could check the HR portal or ask a manager if they needed specifics. For more complex matters, it offered a link to the #HR channel or an email address.

After building five or six topics around HR's top questions, Sarah tested the bot using the built-in "Test Chat." She typed "How do I get maternity leave?" The bot recognized "maternity" as part of the "Maternity or Parental Leave" topic, displaying a short policy summary and linking a relevant form. Satisfied, Sarah published the bot to the Teams channel—creating a new app manifest that put "HRHelperBot" in the company's app store.

Once posted, Sarah pinned a short message: "Meet HRHelperBot! Ask it about time off, benefits, address changes, and more. If it can't help, it'll direct you to the right person." The HR manager was delighted—within days, fewer people interrupted them with routine questions. Some employees typed random queries, but the bot politely answered or referred them to a general FAQ. Over time, Sarah refined the bot's topics to handle synonyms or expand on partial queries.

The success spurred interest in other departments. Could a "HelpDeskBot" handle IT inquiries like "How do I reset my password?" or "Which VPN client do we use?" Sarah realized the same approach applied: gather top FAQs, build topics, and integrate escalation paths. The immediate reduction in HR staff's day-to-day overhead proved the bot's worth. They could now devote energy to deeper HR issues instead of copying and pasting policy answers. For Sarah, it was another example of the Power Platform's ability to empower non-tech employees—giving them a user-friendly solution that lived where everyone already worked: Teams.

Power Virtual Agents extends Teams into the realm of conversational interfaces, letting you build chatbots for FAQs, helpdesk triage, or even data retrieval tasks. With a little planning around topics, triggers, and possible escalation, you can craft a bot that saves time and fosters self-service. The next steps often involve hooking the bot into external systems via Power Automate, enabling advanced tasks like checking a CRM record or logging a support ticket.

As Sarah's HR FAQ bot shows, clear use cases and ongoing refinement are keys to success. A well-targeted bot quickly gains traction if it genuinely helps employees find answers or complete tasks. In our upcoming chapters, we'll further explore how to manage these advanced solutions—covering security, data governance, and scaling your app ecosystem. But for now, if you're eager to lighten a repetitive Q&A load, a Teams chatbot might just be your next big win.

CHAPTER 8: GOVERNANCE AND SECURITY FOR APPS

Embracing apps and integrations in Microsoft Teams can supercharge productivity—but it also introduces questions about who can install them, how data is accessed, and whether certain tools might breach company policies. That's where governance comes in, ensuring that while employees innovate with new apps, the organization maintains control and meets security or compliance requirements. In this chapter, we'll discuss setting up governance policies for Teams apps, exploring how to manage data and permissions at both the tenant and team levels. We'll wrap up with a look at Sarah's experiences at 365 Strategies, where she helps craft a balanced policy that satisfies both enthusiastic "app champions" and cautious IT stakeholders.

A Teams environment without guardrails can become the "wild west"— users installing countless apps, some of which might request broad permissions or store data in unknown servers. A strict lockdown can stifle innovation, forcing employees to rely on older methods. Governance is about striking a middle ground—defining who can approve apps, monitoring how data flows, and keeping track of usage. This chapter isn't about shutting down all new tools; it's about protecting your organization while still letting teams benefit from the power of integrations.

By default, smaller organizations might let every user install apps from the Teams App Store, trusting that employees make sensible choices. But in larger or more regulated settings, you might prefer to limit that power. For instance:

- User-Level Consent: If your environment is relaxed, each user can add an app that requires minimal permissions. This fosters easy experimentation but can lead to many unknown apps in different teams.

- Admin Approval: Some businesses require an admin or designated "app approver" to review each new app. Employees trying to install a new app see a message that approval is needed. The admin checks the app's compliance, data usage, and security rating before approving or rejecting.

You can also define roles—like a "Team Owner" can add certain apps, but a standard "Member" cannot. Or you might create a small "App Governance" group in IT that reviews requests and decides which apps are permitted globally or restricted to certain teams. This approach keeps the environment organized and prevents accidental use of unvetted integrations.

Approving an app once isn't the end of the story. If the tool later changes ownership or updates its permissions, you may need to re-check it. A governance policy typically outlines how often to review installed apps—quarterly or biannually, for example—and who will do the review. During these audits, you might:

- Look for apps with zero usage (removing them to reduce clutter).

- Confirm that data access is still appropriate for each app's current version.

- Revoke certain apps if the vendor no longer meets your security standards.

Many organizations rely on the Teams admin center and usage reports to see how frequently an app is used, which channels it appears in, and whether any new permissions have been requested. This data-driven approach ensures your policies remain flexible. If an app sees widespread beneficial use, you might promote it as a recommended tool. If it's rarely touched, perhaps it's time to retire it.

When your employees connect a third-party app, that tool might read or write channel messages, access files, or track user data. A basic connector, for instance, might only post notifications when an event happens in a linked SaaS platform. But a more advanced app could read the entire chat history, searching for keywords or storing content externally. This raises data protection concerns—especially under regulations like the General Data Protection Regulation (GDPR) in Europe or HIPAA in U.S. healthcare.

A governance policy typically classifies apps into categories:

- Low Risk: Minimal data usage, read-only or notifications.

- Medium Risk: Apps that may store some user data but remain within recognized providers or secure environments.

- High Risk: Apps that request broad chat or file access, or that transfer data to unverified external locations.

Depending on the category, you might set stricter approval processes or additional security reviews. Some organizations maintain a "whitelist" of apps that are pre-approved, a "greylist" requiring IT sign-off, and a "blacklist" that's outright blocked.

If you operate in regulated sectors, you'll need to confirm that integrated apps also comply with relevant laws. A healthcare provider must ensure that patient data or conversation logs that contain personal health information (PHI) stay within HIPAA guidelines. Similarly, GDPR mandates that EU residents' personal data is stored or processed lawfully. Some third-party apps might not guarantee data residency in a particular region. If the app's data flow violates local requirements, your compliance team might forbid it.

You can also rely on Microsoft's own compliance frameworks. The Microsoft 365 compliance center tracks which data is stored where, and many first-party apps are covered by Microsoft's compliance offerings. Third-party vendors often publish security documentation or sign business associate agreements (BAAs) for healthcare compliance. As part of your governance process, gather this documentation before approving an app for widespread use.

In large enterprises, you might have hundreds or thousands of Teams across different departments. Each one might have unique needs for apps. However, managing each team individually can be a nightmare. Instead, you can apply tenant-wide app permission policies that define whether a certain app is:

- Allowed (usable by all).

- Blocked (no one can add it).

- Available with admin approval (users request it, admin decides).

This approach offers global oversight. For instance, you might allow common productivity apps like Planner, Trello, or Polly but block ephemeral chat tools that store data in unknown servers. If a department wants a specialized app, they request an exception. The Teams admin center's policy setup ensures these rules apply consistently across the entire tenant, so any new team or channel automatically inherits them.

The Teams admin center is your command post for policies. You can create multiple app permission policies:

- A "Default Policy" for most staff, allowing standard Microsoft apps and well-known third-party ones.

- A "Restricted Policy" for high-security departments (like Finance or Legal), blocking all but a handful of critical integrations.

- A "Developer Policy" that might let a test group or IT users side-load or build custom apps.

Each policy is assigned to user groups. If your finance staff is assigned the "Restricted Policy," they can't install apps beyond what's pre-approved. Meanwhile, your marketing staff, assigned the "Default Policy," can explore a wider range of creative tools. The admin center also supports "App Setup Policies," controlling how the app icons appear in the Teams sidebar or pinned at the top for quick access.

Crafting a Governance Policy at 365 Strategies

Over the past months, Sarah introduced several new apps—like a polling tool and a Trello integration. Other departments started requesting apps for scheduling, design feedback, or specialized analytics. One day, the IT director approached her: "We need a formal governance policy. Some departments are installing random tools that could pose a risk or conflict with compliance rules. Could you help draft guidelines to strike a balance between freedom and security?"

Sarah teamed up with an IT security lead and a representative from HR. Together, they mapped a straightforward policy:

1. Default Allowed List: Microsoft's own apps (Planner, Forms, Power BI, etc.) plus widely used third-party tools with proven security records (Trello, Polly, Asana).

2. Admin Approval: For lesser-known apps, the user must submit a short request form—explaining why they need it and how it handles data. An IT approver reviews the vendor's compliance statement.

3. Blocked Category: Any app that requests advanced permissions (like reading all channel messages) or lacks a clear privacy policy. The policy can be revisited if the vendor updates their security stance.

They also set quarterly reviews. The IT lead would check usage logs for each installed app, removing any that had zero usage or had questionable updates. The finance department insisted on a minimal approach for their own channels, so they used the Teams admin center to apply a "Restricted Apps" policy to that user group.

When they announced this policy, a few employees grumbled: "Now it's harder to experiment!" But Sarah communicated the benefits: "We still encourage new tools if they fill a gap. You just need a quick approval so we ensure no compliance red flags. If it passes, you can keep using it." She used the example of the HR FAQ bot—someone had suggested a third-party Q&A app, but after a quick check, they decided a custom Power Virtual Agent was safer and just as good.

Within a month, the new governance plan felt natural. Colleagues appreciated that they could see an "Approved Apps" list, making them confident about data safety. And the IT team relaxed because they had a clear process to assess risk. Sarah was pleased: from her vantage point in marketing, users could still find and propose useful tools, but there was a standard protocol for verifying them. This approach let 365 Strategies embrace the richness of the Teams ecosystem without drifting into chaos or compliance nightmares.

A robust governance framework keeps your Microsoft Teams environment both innovative and secure. By defining who can install or approve apps, consistently reviewing usage, and tailoring permission policies across different user groups, you create an environment that encourages exploration while safeguarding data. Regulatory considerations, especially in industries with strict compliance rules, demand careful oversight of third-party apps, ensuring they don't handle sensitive information improperly.

As Sarah's story shows, governance doesn't have to crush creativity—rather, it acts as a guided structure. Employees know which apps are readily available and which require extra checks. Admins stay on top of usage, removing old or risky tools. And once everyone sees how well-chosen apps benefit productivity, they accept a bit of due diligence as part of a healthy ecosystem. In upcoming chapters, we'll explore more advanced scenarios like custom app development and enterprise-scale automation. But remember: none of these flourish without a thoughtful governance plan. By striking the right balance, your organization can confidently expand Teams with new integrations that serve everyone's needs securely.

CHAPTER 9: CUSTOM APP DEVELOPMENT WITH THE TEAMS DEVELOPER PORTAL

Imagine having a tool that lets you build your own apps right inside Microsoft Teams—apps that solve unique problems in your organization, tailored exactly to your needs. Whether it's a specialized time-tracking tool, a custom helpdesk system, or a dashboard for sales data, the Teams Developer Portal gives you the power to create, configure, and distribute custom apps. In this chapter, we'll introduce you to the Teams Developer Portal, explain how to set up bots, connectors, and messaging extensions, and show you how to extend Teams with custom code using the Microsoft Bot Framework and Teams Toolkit. We'll also cover how to test, deploy, and manage these apps over their lifecycle. Finally, we'll follow Sarah as she works with a software developer to create a simple time-tracking app, experiencing the full process from design to deployment—all within Teams.

The Teams Developer Portal is your starting point for building custom applications for Microsoft Teams. It's a web-based interface that lets you create and configure apps that can live as tabs, bots, or connectors right inside Teams. Think of it as a workshop where you assemble all the parts—branding, settings, and features—of your custom app.

Every Teams app has a manifest file—a JSON document that tells Teams about your app. This file defines things like your app's name, icons, description, and the permissions it needs. The Developer Portal guides you through creating a new manifest and helps you upload your app's branding, such as logos and color schemes, so your app feels like a natural part of your company's look and feel.

Once your app is set up, you decide how it will be distributed. You can publish it to your organization's app store, making it available to specific teams or even the entire company. This means that if your custom time-tracking app works well for one department, it can be rolled out to others with just a few clicks.

The Developer Portal also lets you add interactive elements to your app. You can set up a bot that interacts with users through conversation. For example, a bot could answer frequently asked questions or help users fill out a form. Connectors allow your app to receive updates from external systems and post them in a Teams channel, while messaging extensions let users take actions directly from the message box—like pulling data from another service or sharing an interactive card. These tools make your app not only look good but also interact intelligently with your team.

While many apps can be built using templates and the drag-and-drop interface of Power Apps, sometimes you need custom code to solve a specific problem. This is where the Microsoft Bot Framework and Teams Toolkit come into play.

The Microsoft Bot Framework is a set of tools and libraries that help you build complex bots with custom conversation logic. With it, you can write code in languages like C# or JavaScript to handle user input, process data, and interact with external APIs. The Teams Toolkit simplifies the process by providing pre-built templates and integrations that make it easier to create bots specifically for Teams.

For example, if you need a bot that checks your organization's internal database for employee time entries or project updates, you can write a custom script using the Bot Framework. The toolkit then packages your bot so that it can be deployed as part of a Teams app. The result is an app that feels seamless to users but does a lot of heavy lifting in the background.

Many companies have internal systems—like CRM tools, time-tracking systems, or inventory management software—that are critical to their operations. Custom apps built with Power Apps and enhanced with custom code can bridge these systems with Teams. Imagine a scenario where your sales team needs real-time data from your CRM while on a call; a custom-built bot could query the CRM and post key statistics in the chat. Alternatively, if your finance department needs a streamlined way to record expenses or log invoice approvals, a custom Power App could do that, linking directly to your accounting software.

This kind of integration means you don't have to switch between multiple platforms. Everything happens within Teams, and your custom app can be tailored precisely to your business processes. The flexibility of custom code means that even unique or very specific workflows can be automated, saving time and reducing manual errors.

Before rolling out any custom app to the entire organization, it's important to test it thoroughly. The Teams Developer Portal lets you publish your app to a development environment where a small group of users can try it out. During this pilot phase, you can gather feedback, identify bugs, and fine-tune the app's functionality. Testing might involve checking the app on different devices (desktop, mobile, web), ensuring that it interacts correctly with external systems, and confirming that permissions are set correctly so only authorized users can access sensitive data.

Once your app passes testing, you can deploy it more broadly. You have options: roll it out to a specific team, a department, or across the whole company. This decision might depend on the app's purpose and sensitivity. For a tool like a time-tracking app, you might start with one department that's willing to try something new, then use their success as a case study for wider rollout. Deployment is handled via the Teams admin center, where you assign the app to specific user groups or set up a tenant-wide policy. Updates, bug fixes, and improvements can then be rolled out as new versions, following a clear app lifecycle from development to production.

Prototyping a Custom Contact Directory App

At 365 Strategies, Sarah noticed that many employees, especially in the marketing department, struggled to quickly find contact information for colleagues in different teams. Email directories were outdated, and many were stored in separate systems that required extra steps to access. Remembering a recent Power Apps workshop, Sarah decided it was time to build a custom contact directory app that could be embedded directly in Teams.

Sarah teamed up with a software developer from the IT department. Together, they set up a simple canvas app using Power Apps Studio. Sarah started by defining the essential fields: Name, Department, Email, Phone Extension, and a small photo. They connected the app to a SharePoint list where HR maintained up-to-date contact information. The developer used the Teams Toolkit to package the app, ensuring it met all technical requirements.

Once the prototype was ready, Sarah embedded the app as a tab in the marketing channel. Within minutes, her teammates could click on the "Contact Directory" tab and search for colleagues using a simple search box. The interface was clean and intuitive—no more scrolling through outdated directories or switching between apps.

Colleagues were impressed. One team member commented, "This is exactly what we needed—everything in one place." Sarah's pilot showed that even non-developers could benefit from a custom app that addressed a real need. The success of the contact directory encouraged Sarah to consider other custom solutions, like an app for tracking campaign approvals or managing internal asset requests.

Her experience demonstrated that building custom apps in Teams isn't just for tech experts—it's accessible to anyone with a good idea and the willingness to learn a few new tools. The collaboration between business users and IT led to a solution that boosted productivity and made everyday tasks simpler.

Custom app development with the Teams Developer Portal empowers you to tailor Microsoft Teams to your organization's unique needs. Whether you're creating a simple contact directory or a complex workflow that integrates with your line-of-business systems, the process begins with understanding your goals, choosing the right development model (canvas vs. model-driven), and testing thoroughly before wide rollout. The flexibility of custom code, combined with the power of low-code tools, means that even non-developers can contribute to a richer, more efficient collaborative workspace.

Sarah's journey—from the initial idea to prototyping, testing, and finally deploying a contact directory app—shows that with a bit of creativity and collaboration, you can significantly reduce manual work and improve how information flows within your organization. As you move forward, you'll learn how to refine these apps, manage their lifecycles, and integrate them even more deeply with Teams' overall ecosystem.

CHAPTER 10: SHOWCASING SUCCESS AND LOOKING AHEAD

As you reach the final chapter of this book, it's time to reflect on the transformative power of integrating apps into Microsoft Teams and to look forward to what the future holds. In today's fast-paced work environment, many companies have leveraged custom apps and integrations to dramatically improve efficiency, boost productivity, and enhance collaboration. In this chapter, we'll examine real-world case studies that demonstrate how businesses have reaped these benefits, explore practical methods to measure return on investment (ROI) and user satisfaction, and discuss emerging trends—like AI-driven features and advanced Power Platform capabilities—that promise to take Teams apps to the next level.

Across industries, organizations have found that integrating apps directly into Teams can solve persistent problems. For instance, some companies have streamlined their project management by embedding task boards and time trackers, ensuring that every team member sees updates in real time without needing to switch between multiple platforms. Others have used custom approval workflows to automate routine tasks, such as document sign-offs and expense reimbursements. These case studies reveal a common thread: by reducing the need for manual processes, organizations are saving time, reducing errors, and ultimately creating a smoother workflow.

Consider a mid-sized marketing agency that implemented a custom project dashboard using Power BI integrated as a tab in Teams. This dashboard pulled real-time data from their CRM and project management tools, providing a live snapshot of campaign performance. As a result, managers could quickly spot trends and adjust strategies on the fly, leading to better-informed decisions and faster turnaround times on client projects. Meanwhile, a global consulting firm adopted a combination of Planner and Power Automate to handle expense approvals and scheduling across multiple time zones. Their automated flows reduced paperwork and eliminated the delays that once plagued cross-regional communication.

These examples also come with lessons learned. Some companies discovered that a rushed implementation—without proper testing or user training—could lead to underutilized apps or miscommunication. Others found that not setting clear guidelines for app usage led to a cluttered Teams environment where important notifications were drowned out by less critical updates. The key takeaway is that thoughtful planning and ongoing review are essential. Successful organizations create a roadmap for app integration that includes pilot testing, regular audits, and continuous feedback from users.

To justify the time and expense of building custom apps and integrating third-party solutions, it's vital to measure both the return on investment and how satisfied users are with these tools. One effective strategy is tracking app usage metrics: How often are the apps opened? Which tabs do users interact with most? What percentage of a team's workflow is now automated compared to the previous manual processes?

Surveys and feedback forms can also provide qualitative insights. Asking employees how much time they've saved, whether they find the tools intuitive, and what improvements they'd like to see can guide further development. For example, a company might track that after implementing a custom approval flow, the average document review time dropped from several hours to just under 30 minutes. This not only boosts productivity but also enhances employee morale, as staff can focus on creative, high-value tasks instead of repetitive manual work.

Beyond internal metrics, some organizations integrate app usage data with overall performance indicators—like project completion rates or customer satisfaction scores—to paint a broader picture of how these integrations impact business outcomes. Regularly reviewing these metrics helps ensure that the app ecosystem evolves with user needs and that any underperforming apps are either improved or phased out.

The world of digital collaboration is in constant flux, and Microsoft Teams is at the forefront of that evolution. One of the most exciting trends is the integration of AI-driven features. Microsoft's upcoming Copilot and other intelligent assistants are set to revolutionize how meetings, chat, and workflows are managed. Imagine a scenario where AI automatically summarizes your Teams meeting, extracts key action items, and even suggests follow-up tasks based on the conversation. This not only saves time but also helps ensure that no critical details are missed.

In addition to AI, expect to see deeper integrations with the broader Power Platform. Enhanced Power Apps and Power Automate capabilities will allow organizations to build even more sophisticated, low-code solutions that run seamlessly within Teams. Future developments may also include advanced natural language processing for bots, improved custom connectors for specialized business systems, and even more granular security controls that protect sensitive data while facilitating collaboration.

The trend toward unified communications continues, as Teams evolves to blend voice, chat, file sharing, and app integrations into one coherent experience. With every update, Microsoft aims to reduce the friction between disparate tools, helping users accomplish more without having to leave the Teams environment. As a result, organizations can expect a future where digital workflows are not only automated and intelligent but also more personalized and responsive to the needs of individual users.

Sarah's Story

At 365 Strategies, Sarah had been a driving force in adopting and fine-tuning the company's Teams app ecosystem. Over the past months, she had witnessed firsthand how various integrations—ranging from custom dashboards to automated approval flows—had transformed daily operations. Now, Sarah was tasked with compiling a set of success stories for an internal presentation on the ROI of these Teams apps.

Sarah began by gathering data: she reviewed analytics from the Teams admin center and Power BI dashboards, noting improvements like reduced approval times and increased engagement in project channels. She also interviewed colleagues who had benefited from these integrations. One department had completely eliminated lengthy email chains for expense approvals, while another found that real-time dashboards allowed them to spot and address issues almost immediately.

Inspired by these insights, Sarah organized the stories into a concise presentation. She highlighted how a custom project dashboard not only saved time but also improved decision-making. She showcased the automated approval flows that had cut document review times significantly, and she even shared anecdotes from teams that had become more agile as a result of these new tools.

Then came the most exciting part: during a recent Microsoft briefing, Sarah learned about upcoming AI-driven features, including Copilot. The briefing revealed how future Teams apps might automatically transcribe meetings, extract key points, and even flag urgent tasks. Sarah's eyes lit up at the possibility. She shared her enthusiasm with her team, proposing a pilot program to test these new AI features as soon as they became available.

Her presentation resonated widely within the company, sparking conversations about further innovation and encouraging other departments to share their own success stories. Colleagues began to see the Power Platform not just as a collection of isolated tools, but as an integrated ecosystem that was steadily driving the company's overall efficiency. Sarah's work had demonstrated that when you measure ROI not just in dollars saved but in time and improved communication, the future of Teams apps looks incredibly promising.

In this chapter, we've explored how real-world case studies, user feedback, and emerging technologies shape the future of Teams apps. By measuring ROI and tracking user satisfaction, organizations can pinpoint which integrations deliver true value and which need adjustment. As Microsoft continues to invest in AI-driven features and advanced Power Platform capabilities, the potential for even smarter, more responsive workflows will grow.

Sarah's journey—compiling success stories, presenting compelling data, and getting excited about new AI tools—illustrates the dynamic evolution of digital collaboration. Her experience shows that with careful planning, continual optimization, and a willingness to embrace emerging technologies, your organization can build a vibrant, integrated app ecosystem in Microsoft Teams.

Looking ahead, the future of Teams apps is bright. Whether you're already using a range of integrations or just beginning to explore the possibilities, remember that every innovation is part of a broader movement toward unified, intelligent communication. And if you're hungry for more insights, the Microsoft Teams Companion Series has additional volumes covering telephony, channels, chats, custom app development, and more. Your journey to a fully integrated, modern workplace continues—one app, one workflow, and one success story at a time.

UNITING APPS AND INTEGRATIONS FOR A SMARTER WORKSPACE

As we reach the end of our journey into the world of apps and integrations in Microsoft Teams, it's clear that the power to transform your daily work doesn't just lie in isolated features—it comes from unifying all your essential tools in one seamless environment. Throughout this book, we've explored how embedding apps like OneNote, Lists, Power BI, and many others into Teams can drastically reduce context-switching, streamline workflows, and keep all your project data at your fingertips. We've seen how customizations—whether through built-in app tabs, messaging extensions, or even developing your own solutions with Power Apps, Power Automate, and Power Virtual Agents—can address the unique challenges your organization faces.

Our discussion began with an exploration of why apps and integrations matter. In a world where employees once toggled between endless browser tabs, separate platforms, and disjointed tools, integrating these functionalities into Teams makes collaboration smoother and more intuitive. By bringing familiar Microsoft 365 applications into the heart of your team's communication, you create a centralized hub where documents, dashboards, and conversations coexist seamlessly. You learn not only to access these tools but also to customize them—pinning critical documents as tabs, creating shortcuts in the message composer, and even embedding real-time dashboards that let you see live data without leaving the chat.

We then ventured into the Teams App Store, discovering how to navigate its vast catalog, filter apps by category, and understand the permissions and consents required for each integration. With real-world examples like Planner, Trello, Polly, and Forms, you've seen how popular apps can address everyday needs while industry-specific extensions provide tailored solutions for fields like healthcare or finance.

The key takeaway was that effective app adoption isn't about flooding your workspace with every tool under the sun—it's about selecting the right apps that solve real problems and rolling them out thoughtfully, with proper training and onboarding.

The journey continued with built-in apps and customization. You learned how to leverage the full suite of Microsoft 365 tools—like OneNote for capturing meeting ideas, Excel for dynamic spreadsheets, and SharePoint libraries for organized file storage—right within Teams. Customizing your workspace not only makes it easier for team members to access what they need but also minimizes the risk of information getting lost or outdated. By embedding dashboards, you create a real-time window into your team's performance, ensuring everyone stays aligned with the latest data.

Next, we dived into the Power Platform—a collection of tools that truly empowers any organization to build custom solutions without extensive coding. With Power Automate, you can create workflows that automatically send notifications, trigger approval processes, and even generate daily summaries. Power Apps lets you design bespoke applications that address specific business challenges, while Power Virtual Agents bring conversational interfaces to your channels, handling routine queries and freeing up valuable time for your staff. The examples and case studies illustrated how even simple automations can reduce repetitive tasks and increase overall efficiency.

Sarah's journey has been our constant companion through these chapters. We've followed her as she transformed scattered processes into unified workflows. From her initial discovery of the Teams App Store—where she quickly realized that a polling app like Polly could eliminate confusing email threads—to building a custom contact directory that saved her colleagues from the hassle of outdated spreadsheets, Sarah's experiences illustrate that innovation is within everyone's reach. Her experiments with Power Automate not only streamlined her team's project updates but also demonstrated that a few well-designed flows can transform repetitive manual tasks into automated, error-free processes. And when she built an HR FAQ bot with Power Virtual Agents, she proved that even non-developers can create useful tools that lighten the load on support teams.

By integrating these apps, customizations, and automation tools into Teams, you're not just adding features—you're building a cohesive, intelligent ecosystem that evolves with your business needs. The benefits are clear: increased productivity, reduced reliance on multiple disparate tools, and a smoother, more engaging workflow that keeps your team focused on high-value work.

Looking ahead, the future of Teams apps is incredibly promising. Emerging AI-driven features—like Microsoft's upcoming Copilot—are poised to further revolutionize how we manage meetings, transcribe conversations, and extract actionable insights automatically. As Microsoft continues to expand the Power Platform, expect even deeper integrations and more powerful low-code/no-code developments that make custom solutions easier than ever to build and deploy. This evolution of unified communications means that every interaction, whether it's a quick chat, a detailed meeting, or a comprehensive project update, becomes part of a seamless, data-rich experience.

If you've enjoyed this exploration of apps and integrations, the journey doesn't end here. The Microsoft Teams Companion Series offers additional volumes that dive into every facet of Teams, ensuring you have the right tools to master your digital workspace:

- Introduction to Microsoft Teams lays the groundwork for licensing, setup, and user roles.

- Teams & Channels explores how to organize people and projects effectively.

- Chats & Meetings details best practices for real-time communication.

- Teams Phones guides you through telephony and voice solutions.

- Copilot in Microsoft Teams delves into AI-driven features for smarter collaboration.

- Accessibility in Microsoft Teams focuses on creating inclusive workspaces.

- Microsoft Teams in Education tailors Teams for teachers, students, and academic institutions.

- Security, Compliance, and Administration covers advanced governance and enterprise-level management.

- Expert Tips & Troubleshooting offers power-user hacks and solutions to common issues.

Each book in the series is written in an easy-to-understand style, complete with real-world examples and Sarah's ongoing adventures to illustrate how these concepts translate into practical improvements. Whether you're an IT professional, a business leader, or simply someone looking to boost productivity, the series will guide you step by step in transforming your workplace into a modern, integrated collaboration hub.

The integration of apps within Microsoft Teams is not merely a technical upgrade—it's a strategic enhancement that unites all your work tools into one cohesive system. As you implement these custom solutions and automate repetitive tasks, remember that every change brings you closer to a more efficient, data-driven, and user-friendly environment. Sarah's journey shows us that with creativity, thoughtful planning, and a bit of experimentation, even complex tools can become indispensable parts of your daily workflow.

Embrace the future of Teams by exploring, testing, and continuously refining your app ecosystem. With the right balance of innovation and governance, your organization can achieve a unified, intelligent workspace where every app, every flow, and every conversation contributes to a smarter, more productive tomorrow.